BE SAFE! BE SAFE! BE SAFE! BE SAFE! BE SAFE! BE SAF
SAFE! BE SAFE! BE SAFE! BE SAFE! BE SAFE! BE SAFE! BE S
FE! BE SAFE! BE SAFE! BE SAFE! BE SAFE! BE SAFE! BE SAF
SAFE! BE SAFE! BE SAFE! BE SAFE! BE S
FE! BE SAFE! BE SAFE! BE SAF
SAFE! BE SAFE! BE BE S.
FE! BE SAFE! BE SAFE F SAF
SAFE! BE SAFE! BE SA !: BE S.
FE! BE SAFE! BE SAFE! AFE! BE SAFE! BE SAF
SAFE! BE SAFE! BE SAFE! BE SAFE! BE SAFE! BE SAFE! BE S.
FE! BE SAFE! BE SAFE! BE SAFE! BE SAFE! BE SAFE! BE SAF
SAFE! BE SAFE! BE SAFE! BE SAFE! BE SAFE! BE SAFE! BE S.
FE! BE SAFE! BE SAFE! BE SAFE! BE SAFE! BE SAFE! BE SAF
SAFE! BE SAFE! BE SAFE! BE SAFE! BE SAFE! BE SAFE! BE S.
FE! BE SAFE! BE SAFE! BE SAFE! BE SAFE! BE SAFE! BE SAF
SAFE! BE SAFE! BE SAFE! BE SAFE! BE SAFE! BE SAFE! BE S
FE! BE SAFE! BE SAFE! BE SAFE! BE SAFE! BE SAFE! BE SAF
SAFE! BE SAFE! BE SAFE! BE SAFE! BE SAFE! BE SAFE! BE S
FE! BE SAFE! BE SAFE! BE SAFE! BE SAFE! BE SAFE! BE SAF
SAFE! BE SAFE! BE SAFE! BE SAFE! BE SAFE! BE SAFE! BE S.
FE! BE SAFE! BE SAFE! BE SAFE! BE SAFE! BE SAFE! BE SAF
SAFE! BE SAFE! BE SAFE! BE SAFE! BE SAFE! BE SAFE! BE S.
FE! BE SAFE! BE SAFE! BE SAFE! BE SAFE! BE SAFE! BE SAF
SAFE! BE SAFE! BE SAFE! BE SAFE! BE SAFE! BE SAFE! BE S.
FE! BE SAFE! BE SAFE! BE SAFE! BE SAFE! BE SAFE! BE SAF
SAFE! BE SAFE! BE SAFE! BE SAFE! BE SAFE! BE SAFE! BE S.

D0394523

BE SAFE!

BE SAFE!

SIMPLE STRATEGIES FOR
DEATH-FREE
LIVING

QUIRK BOOKS

PHILADELPHIA

Copyright © 2004 by Quirk Productions, Inc.

Library of Congress Cataloging in Publication Number: 2004103015

ISBN: 1-931686-71-8

Printed in Singapore

Typeset in Akzidenz Grotesk and Optima

Designed by Karen Onorato
Illustrations by Willie Ryan

Distributed in North America by Chronicle Books
85 Second Street
San Francisco, CA 94105

10 9 8 7 6 5 4 3 2 1

Quirk Books
215 Church Street
Philadelphia, PA 19106
www.quirkbooks.com

NG

Chapter 1: Around the House
What Is the Safest . . .

Chapter 2: In the Kitchen
What Is the Safest . . .

Chapter 3: Food and Drink
What Is the Safest . . .

Chapter 4: In the Bathroom
What Is the Safest . . .

Chapter 5: Man's Best Friend
What Is the Safest . . .

Chapter 6: Sports and Entertainment
What Is the Safest . . .

Chapter 7: Travel and the Great Outdoors

What Is the Safest . . .

Chapter 8: Planes, Trains, and Automobiles

What Is the Safest . . .

Chapter 9: Everyday Safety

What Is the Safest . . .

EVERYTHING CAN BE DANGEROUS.

The littlest things in our everyday lives can have injurious or even deadly results. Tomorrow, you could catch hepatitis from a toothbrush. You could crash your car on the way to work. You could be killed at a baseball game.

At a dinner party, do you know how to make sure the hors d'oeuvres won't make your guests sick? In a public bathroom, do you know the cleanest way to dry your hands, or which stall you should choose to best avoid germs? And when you sleep in a motel, do you know how to avoid catching anything from the person who slept there before you? And I do mean *anything* (see page 76).

If not, then this book is for you. Here's how to avoid the pitfalls of everyday living—how to stay safe in a world where *everything* is dangerous. And while there's no way to completely safeguard your life, there is always a safer way to do things.

Before I started writing this book, I was, for the most part, a normal person with slight, perhaps somewhat magnified, anxieties about things like touching the handles of public toilets and drinking the milk after my roommate takes a swig directly from the carton.

In the beginning, my research made me worry even more. Should I stop eating sushi? Should I even use public bathrooms? Should I throw away all my dishware and go for paper plates to avoid using that dreaded kitchen sponge?

But then my paranoia started to evolve into something else: awareness. Because I've realized that it's all about being aware of your own choices. Simple choices can make all the difference—the seat you choose on the subway, the lane you choose on the highway, the place you sit at a base-ball game.

I'm not saying you should go out and buy gas masks, eat only canned food (which, by the way, isn't so safe anyway [see page 30]), and avoid crossing the street on Saturdays. Go about your life. But know when and how to make good decisions. Be aware of when your choices matter, and when they make a difference.

Because everything can be dangerous, and all you can do is try to be safe.

Now go wash your hands.

CHAPTER 1

AROUND THE HOUSE

WHAT IS THE SAFEST POSITION FOR TV WATCHING?

AT LEAST 6 TO 8 FEET FROM THE SCREEN.

WHY? Contrary to those old wives' tales, sitting too close to the television won't permanently damage your eyesight or expose you to radiation; it may, however, cause temporary eye fatigue and eye-strain (which can usually be relieved by a good night's sleep). While some television sets built before 1968 actually did emit potentially damaging X-rays, all TVs built since then are completely safe.

⚠ **WORDS OF CAUTION:** *Don't watch television in a completely dark room. This can also contribute to eye fatigue.*

WHAT IS THE SAFEST NUMBER OF APPLIANCES TO PLUG INTO AN EXTENSION CORD?

ONE.

WHY? Extension cords are intended only to extend your range—they are not designed to provide you with additional outlets. All extension cords have a wattage rating, and plugging in multiple appliances will create a demand above that amount. Overloading extension cords can cause fires. Read the rating on the label and be sure you're using the proper gauge cord for the appliance you want to power. If you absolutely must plug in more than one appliance, add up the wattage and be sure the total doesn't exceed the cord's rating.

⚠ *WORDS OF CAUTION: Never connect multiple extension cords; this increases the risk of sparking. Use a power strip instead: It can handle several appliances at a time because it is designed to shut off automatically if too much wattage is demanded.*

WHAT IS THE SAFEST KIND OF LANDLINE PHONE?

A CORDED PHONE.

WHY? Standard corded phones are essential for safety because they'll work during a power outage. In addition, your privacy is more protected when using this kind of phone. Cordless phones are safer only in the event of a lightning storm (see page 83).

⚠ **WORDS OF CAUTION:** *Be careful what you say when you're on a cordless phone, especially when relaying credit card or bank account information. Anyone with a radio scanner—or a baby monitor, a walkie-talkie, or just another cordless phone—can pick up on your conversations. Cordless phones that operate on higher frequencies (902 MHz) are a little better, particularly those that use digital technology.*

WHAT IS THE SAFEST POSITION FOR SLEEPING?

ON YOUR SIDE, WITH YOUR KNEES BENT.

WHY? This position takes the most stress off the back and allows for easy breathing. Experts say sleeping on the left side in particular can help ward off heartburn.

⚠ *WORDS OF CAUTION: Do not sleep on your stomach. This position hyperextends the whole back and forces you to twist your neck to the side at an unnatural angle. If you are unable to sleep in a different position, experts recommend putting a pillow under your stomach to help straighten out the spine.*

NO HIGHER THAN THE THIRD RUNG FROM THE TOP, WITH THE LADDER ON A STABLE SURFACE.

WHY? Standing too near the top can make a ladder unstable and lead to its collapse or your downfall. Literally. Each year, more than 300 people die and more than 164,000 are injured after failing to use ladders safely. If the ladder wobbles from side to side, you increase your chances of falling.

⚠️ ***WORDS OF CAUTION:*** *Know your ladder's weight rating and do not exceed it. Most general-use ladders are type III, meaning they can carry up to 200 pounds (90 kg) total. Also, be sure to position the ladder correctly: The bottom should be 1 foot (.3 m) away from the wall for every 4 feet (1.2 m) that the ladder rises. For example, if the ladder touches the wall 16 feet (5 m) above the ground, the bottom of the ladder should be 4 feet (1.2 m) from the wall. Also, if you are going to climb onto a roof, the ladder should extend 3 feet (1 m) higher than the roof.*

WHAT IS THE SAFEST WAY TO HAMMER A NAIL?

BY HOLDING THE NAIL WITH A PAIR OF PLIERS.

WHY? According to the U.S. Consumer Product Safety Commission, each year more than 40,000 people are injured using hammers. The top injury? A smashed finger. Holding the nail with pliers allows you to hold the nail steady and avoid crushing your fingers.

⚠ *WORDS OF CAUTION:* *Before you start pounding, check your hammer. Hold the head in one hand and the handle in the other. Try to jiggle the head. If it's loose, don't use it—you don't want the hammerhead flying off mid-swing.*

VEGETABLE OIL (FOR OIL-BASED PAINTS) OR WATER (FOR WATER-BASED PAINTS).

WHY? Using the appropriate solvent for your paint will make the removal process simple—and safe. Paint thinner or turpentine, while effective in removing the paint, are powerful chemicals that can be bad for your health and the environment. For oil-based and latex paint, applying another kind of oil is most effective. Water-based paints react well to a combination of water and soap.

⚠ *WORDS OF CAUTION:* *Paint thinner can cause headaches, confusion, and respiratory distress. Turpentine is even more dangerous—it can cause permanent damage to your kidneys.*

WHAT IS THE SAFEST WAY TO PROTECT YOUR HOME AGAINST BURGLARY?

WITH A MONITORED ALARM SYSTEM THAT HAS A RADIO OR CELLULAR BACKUP.

WHY? The first thing a professional burglar will do before entering a home is cut the phone line, because many alarm systems use the phone line to notify the alarm company or police of a break-in. If a radio or cellular phone serves as a backup notification system, the police will still be notified even if the phone line is cut.

⚠ *WORDS OF CAUTION:* *Lock your doors and windows. Approximately 30 percent of U.S. home burglaries do not involve forced entry. More than half of all U.S. burglaries occur during daylight hours—sometimes while you're home. Morning is big for bank robberies, too (page 102).*

WHAT IS THE SAFEST WAY TO GET RID OF ROACHES?

WITH BORIC ACID POWDER.

WHY? Boric acid, unless ingested in large amounts, is not harmful to people and pets but is deadly to cockroaches. (Boron, its main ingredient, can be found in laundry detergents and toothpastes.) Sprinkle the powder in corners, around baseboards, and under cabinets. The roaches will pick it up as they scamper across the area. The powder draws moisture from their bodies, causing them to die from starvation and dehydration.

⚠ *WORDS OF CAUTION: Boric acid powder should be applied in a very thin layer—roaches will avoid large piles. If the powder gets wet, it loses its ability to kill the roaches; reapply dry powder. Avoid roach sprays, which can be toxic and often contain kerosene, a potential fire hazard and a danger to pets and children if consumed.*

WHAT IS THE SAFEST WAY TO GET RID OF BACKYARD PESTS?

USING URINE-BASED REPELLENTS.

WHY? Urine-based repellents are the powdered urine of the invading animal's predators (mainly coyotes and foxes). Sprinkling the repellent around the yard creates the perception that the area has been marked by these animals, thereby scaring away common pests such as rabbits, woodchucks, raccoons, and deer. The powders are safe to use in small quantities; unlike chemical repellents, they will not harm either your garden or your family.

⚠ **WORDS OF CAUTION:** *Despite gardening myths to the contrary, scattering human hair across your garden is not an effective means of keeping unwanted critters away. Setting out poisons such as snail, fly, gopher, mouse, or rat bait is also a bad idea: They can be extremely dangerous if ingested by your cat or dog.*

WHAT IS THE SAFEST KIND OF LAWN MOWER?

A REEL-BASED MOWER.

WHY? According to the Consumer Product Safety Commission, more than 70,000 people are injured by power mowers—both the seated and walk-behind varieties—each year. A reel mower (the kind your grandfather used to use) has no engine, so it stops when you do. Reel mowers are also better for the environment because they don't release any fumes into the air.

⚠ **WORDS OF CAUTION:** *Never mow the grass when the ground is wet; you're more likely to slip and fall toward the blades of the mower. When mowing an incline, travel down the hill when using a riding mower, but mow across the hill with a walk-behind mower. Always wear protective eye gear and sturdy shoes while mowing, as objects hurled from the mower can travel more than 30 mph (48 km/h).*

CHAPTER 2

IN THE KITCHEN

WHAT IS THE SAFEST TEMPERATURE AT WHICH TO SET YOUR REFRIGERATOR?

40°F (4.6°C) OR BELOW.

WHY? Once temperatures rise above 40°F (4.6°C), bacteria in food begin to multiply rapidly. A lower temperature won't kill the bacteria, but it will prevent them from multiplying. The fewer bacteria there are, the less likely you'll get sick from them. (Bear in mind that a healthy adult can tolerate a hefty dose of germs—not that you want to test your limits.)

⚠ *WORDS OF CAUTION:* *If your fridge does not have a temperature dial, buy a refrigerator/freezer thermometer and place it on the center shelf (not in the door) of the fridge. Check it once a week to make sure the temperature doesn't exceed 40°F (4.6°C). Turn the gauge down as necessary to hold the temperature. If the temperature continues to rise, it may be time for a repair or a new fridge. Remember: Refrigerator door shelves are the warmest parts of the fridge; do not store eggs or milk there.*

WHAT IS THE SAFEST AMOUNT OF TIME TO KEEP LEFTOVERS IN THE REFRIGERATOR?

NO MORE THAN FIVE DAYS, DEPENDING ON THE FOOD.

WHY? The fridge doesn't get rid of bacteria; it just slows it down. If stored food already has something growing in it (which oftentimes it does), the cool temperatures will slow the rate of bacteria growth, but the longer foods are kept, the more opportunity bacteria have to grow to a level that will make you sick. This is not a one-size-fits-all rule, however; different foods spoil at different times, since some foods provide more suitable breeding grounds than others.

In general, bacteria love foods rich in protein, making meats and poultry more likely to be contaminated than bread or fruit. While it is safe to eat a four-day-old burger after you've recooked it to the proper temperature (165°F [74°C]), you probably wouldn't want to—spoiled food smells bad and has lost its signature flavor.

Fridge Time for Leftovers

Raw Meat	1 to 2 days
Luncheon Meat	3 to 5 days (opened package)
Cooked Meat	3 to 4 days
Gravy and Meat Broth	1 to 2 days
Leftover Pizza	3 to 4 days
Cooked Fish and Shellfish	3 to 4 days

⚠ **WORDS OF CAUTION:** *Store foods that spoil quickly in the back of the fridge; it's coldest there. Never assume that foods stored in the freezer are automatically safe. Freezing stops the growth of bacteria, but it does not kill bacteria already present. Once the food is defrosted, any organisms living inside the food will begin to grow.*

WHAT IS THE SAFEST AMOUNT OF TIME TO LET FOOD SIT ON THE COUNTER?

TWO HOURS OR LESS (ONE HOUR IF THE AMBIENT TEMPERATURE IS ABOVE 90°F [32°C]).

WHY? Given longer than two hours, bacteria in the food will start to multiply, regardless of whether the food is raw or cooked. Be especially careful with meat, fish, shellfish, and dairy products; if you're having a dinner party, don't let the shrimp cocktail or cheese dip sit out all night long.

⚠ *WORDS OF CAUTION: Ask for a doggie bag at a restaurant only if you think you'll be able to get your food in the fridge within two hours. If you're picnicking, bring non-perishables or put your food in a cooler with a refrigerator/freezer thermometer. Make sure the temperature remains at 40°F (4.6°C) or below.*

WHAT IS THE SAFEST AMOUNT OF TIME TO STORE CANNED FOODS?

ONE TO FIVE YEARS, DEPENDING ON THE TYPE OF FOOD.

WHY? High-acid foods such as fruit cocktail and pineapple have the shortest shelf life at 12 to 18 months. This is because the acid inside the can will actually begin to break down the food (and eventually, the can) over time. Low-acid foods such as meat, poultry, fish, and most vegetables will keep two to five years, assuming the can is in good condition and has been stored in a cool, dry place.

⚠ **WORDS OF CAUTION:** Discard cans that are dented, leaking, bulging, or rusted. Some bacteria, like the one that causes botulism, thrive in low-acid, low-oxygen environments such as those offered by canned green beans, beets, and corn. Bulges occur when gas is released by the bacteria.

WHAT IS SAFEST WAY TO CLEAN THE KITCHEN COUNTER?

WITH A PAPER TOWEL.

WHY? Kitchens are about four times more germ-ridden than bathrooms, with the average kitchen sink several times dirtier than the average toilet seat. (Public bathrooms are another story altogether; see pages 109–110.) Sponges and dishrags often spread germs rather than wipe them away. Using a paper towel ensures that potentially harmful germs are thrown away with the towel. To sanitize counters, use a solution of 1 teaspoon (5 ml) liquid household bleach per 1 quart (950 ml) of water.

⚠ **WORDS OF CAUTION:** *If you use cloth towels, launder them daily using hot water. Use separate sponges to clean your counters and dishes. Never dry your hands with a towel that was previously used to clean up raw meat, poultry, or seafood juices.*

THREE TO FOUR WEEKS
(IF YOU CLEAN IT EVERY DAY).

WHY? Sponges are one of the most germ-laden objects in households. Ideally, you should throw your sponge out after every use to avoid contaminating your kitchen counters as well as your dishes and silverware, but that's neither realistic nor economically feasable. If you keep your sponges for three to four weeks, wash it daily by putting it in boiling water for at least ten minutes (tossing it in the dishwasher is perfect) or microwaving it for one minute on high to kill bacteria.

NOTE: *It doesn't really matter what kind of sponge you use. Studies have shown that antibacterial sponges don't make a significant difference in the number of germs found in the average kitchen.*

WHAT IS THE SAFEST KIND OF CUTTING BOARD?

A PLASTIC ONE.

WHY? Studies done on cutting boards, both wooden and plastic, have shown an average of 62,000 bacteria per square inch (9,300/sq. cm) of board. But wooden boards are more bacteria-prone, since they usually have more tiny grooves that offer microorganisms opportunities for burrowing. Bacteria can survive in a dormant state inside these small crevices, contaminating foods the next time the board is used. Plastic boards don't have as many cracks that might harbor bacteria, and they can be rinsed off more easily.

⚠ *WORDS OF CAUTION: Consider using one cutting board for foods that will be cooked, such as fish and chicken, and another for ready-to-eat foods, such as bread and fruit. Remember to throw away your plastic board when it begins to show nicks and scratches. Disposable cutting boards, which can be found in grocery stores, are also a safe option.*

AN ABC-RATED (MULTIPURPOSE) EXTINGUISHER.

WHY? Using the wrong kind of fire extinguisher can actually spread rather than extinguish a fire. Extinguishers are rated in four categories—A, B, C, and ABC. The first three are specialized for use on fires involving combustible materials (A), use on flammable liquid fires (B), and use on fires involving energized electrical equipment (C). Only ABC extinguishers work on all three types of fire.

⚠ *WORDS OF CAUTION: Keep your fire extinguisher in the kitchen, the room where most fires start.*

CHAPTER 3

FOOD AND DRINK

WHAT IS THE SAFEST WAY TO DEFROST MEAT?

IN THE REFRIGERATOR.

WHY? Experts say thawing meat, poultry, and seafood in the fridge does the most even job of defrosting and ensures the food is kept sufficiently cold to prevent bacteria growth. Be sure to place the meat on the lowest shelf; putting it any higher may allow juices to drip bacteria onto the foods below.

⚠ *WORDS OF CAUTION: Do not thaw meat in cold water unless you plan on changing the water every 30 minutes. If you neglect the water, bacteria in the meat (or the water) will multiply as the water warms up. Also, never let meat sit on the counter to defrost; bacteria can multiply rapidly at room temperature.*

ON A GAS GRILL (USED OUTDOORS).

WHY? Charcoal grills may make the quintessential blackened, crispy burger, but they're more dangerous than gas grills. Charcoal produces carbon monoxide when it is burned—and if you breathe in too much carbon monoxide, you can die. More than 30 people die and another 400 are injured in the U.S. every year from using charcoal grills inside houses, under tents, and in garages.

All recently manufactured (post-1995) gas grills in the U.S. are equipped with advanced shut-off mechanisms to prevent gas leaks, but gas grills still pose their share of risk. Heed the following tips to ensure safe barbecues.

• Check the tubes that lead into the burner for insects, spiders, or food grease. Use a pipe cleaner or wire to clear a blockage and push it through to the main part of the burner.

• Check grill hoses for cracking, brittleness,

holes, and leaks. Make sure there are no sharp bends in the hose or tubing. Replace scratched or nicked connectors, which can eventually leak gas.

• Place gas hoses as far away from the hot surface as possible, including areas where grease could drip on them. If you can't move the hoses, install a heat shield to protect them.

⚠ **WORDS OF CAUTION:** *If you must use a charcoal grill, only use starter fluids that are specially designed for grills—never use gasoline or kerosene, both of which can cause explosions. Choose an open area away from overhanging trees for your grilling; don't set up the barbecue in a garage, breezeway, carport, porch, or under an awning or any other covering that can catch fire or trap smoke and fumes.*

WHAT IS THE SAFEST WAY TO COOK A HAMBURGER?

WELL DONE (COOKED TO 160°F [71°C]).

WHY? According to the United States Department of Agriculture (USDA), ground meat is more likely to harbor bacteria than other kinds of meat. Any bacteria or viruses that may have been on the surface of the meat (from unsafe handling, for instance) will be distributed throughout the food once ground. The only way to make sure you're not ingesting something that might make you sick is to cook the meat until it reaches 160°F (71°C), to ensure that all bacteria are destroyed. Use a food thermometer for a precise measurement.

⚠ *WORDS OF CAUTION: Just because your hamburger looks done doesn't mean it is. According to the USDA, one out of every four hamburgers turns brown in the middle before it reaches a safe internal temperature. The only way to know for sure whether the meat you're eating is safe is to take its temperature with a food thermometer.*

WHAT IS THE SAFEST KIND OF RAW FISH?

TUNA (UNLESS YOU'RE PREGNANT).

WHY? Fish can harbor parasitic worms, which cause all sorts of stomach problems, from minor cramping to life-threatening illness. Generally, fish that live farther from the shore are less likely to pick up these worms, which thrive in muddy, shallow water. Tuna is a deep-water fish, so it is less likely to be infected. But, as any doctor will tell you, eating raw fish of any kind can make you sick, especially if it's not served properly. Once the fish is on your plate, check to make sure it has a firm texture and its color is bright and shiny, not slimy; anything less could be a sign of decay.

If you're pregnant, don't eat any tuna, shark, swordfish, king mackerel, or tilefish; these fish, raw or cooked, are more likely to contain high levels of mercury, a chemical linked with birth defects. Young children are also susceptible to high levels of mercury and should avoid these fish.

⚠ **WORDS OF CAUTION:** Be especially careful when eating raw eel, mackerel, salmon, shrimp, and catfish, which are more likely to contain parasitic worms. However, virtually all the raw fish served in sushi bars has been frozen long enough to make it safe to eat, and fish that typically harbor parasites are often served cooked. Quite often, these worms (visible to the naked eye) are cut out by sushi chefs—and the resulting fish is fine to eat. To be safe, eat wasabi and ginger with your sushi; both are antiparasitic and may help ward off illness.

Limit oyster consumption to the winter months. The biggest danger with oysters is the bacteria they absorb from the water. In the winter, lower temperatures don't allow for the growth of bacteria, making oysters much safer to eat.

When choosing a sushi or seafood restaurant or a fishmonger, smell the space before ordering anything. Fresh fish should not smell "fishy"; rather, they should have a subtle, sweet smell. It's only when a fish starts to decompose that it begins to smell fishy.

Avoid ordering raw fish on Mondays—most restaurants don't get deliveries on Sundays, and Monday's delivery may or may not arrive by lunchtime, making it anyone's guess how fresh the tuna is inside your spicy tuna roll. Fridays, by contrast, are the best day to fill up on fish. Restaurants get deliveries as close to the weekend as possible to fill consistently heavier demands. Not surprisingly, fresh deliveries lead to fresh fish.

WHAT IS THE SAFEST KIND OF FRUIT?

PINEAPPLE.

WHY? The pineapple's thick skin keeps it safe from external threats, including pesticides, bugs, and surface bacteria. In a study done by the Environmental Working Group, an organization dedicated to food and environmental safety, fewer than 10 percent of pineapples tested positive for pesticide contamination, compared to about 97 percent of nectarine samples and 94 percent of pear samples.

According to the EPA, lab studies show that pesticides can cause health problems, such as birth defects, nerve damage, and cancer, depending on the quantity and type. The U.S. federal government sets limits on how much pesticide can be used on crops to keep them at a level deemed "safe," but there is still debate over just how safe that is. While washing helps eliminate some of the pesticides, it can't get rid of all of them, since some residue is absorbed into the flesh of the fruit or plant.

Of course, the acidity of pineapple can wreak havoc on the stomach and mouths of many people. In this case, opt for bananas or mangoes, both of which also have low pesticide quantities.

⚠ **WORDS OF CAUTION:** *Don't load up on apples, cherries, or peaches, all of which have the highest levels of pesticides.*

While organic-labeled fruits and vegetables are grown and processed using no synthetic fertilizers or pesticides, they're a safety tradeoff. Pesticides rid food of harmful bacteria or other contaminants; without them, food is vulnerable to a whole host of things, including the deadly E. coli *bacteria.*

WHAT IS THE SAFEST KIND OF BOTTLED WATER?

DISTILLED WATER.

WHY? Distilled water—the condensed steam from boiled water—is 100 percent pure (all contaminants separate out of the steam when the water is boiled). The process of distilling ensures that parasites such as *Cryptosporidium parvum*, one of the most common waterborne parasites (and a culprit behind traveler's diarrhea), are removed.

⚠ **WORDS OF CAUTION:** *Just because it's bottled doesn't mean it's safe. In fact, according to a study by the U.S. National Resources Defense Council, about one-fourth of bottled water is actually treated tap water. "Treating" water doesn't make it bacteria free, and bottles labeled "artesian well water," "mineral water," or "spring water" don't guarantee an absence of parasites, since filtering regulations for bottled water are less stringent than those for municipal water systems. In contrast, tap water in most large American cities is required to be disinfected and filtered to remove pathogens and parasites. If you're still worried, boil your water (whether bottled or from the tap) for one minute and you'll be protected from any unwanted ingredients.*

WHAT IS THE SAFEST WAY TO DRINK FROM A SODA CAN?

THROUGH A STRAW, AFTER WIPING OFF THE TOP.

WHY? Studies have shown that most unwashed soda cans are spotted with mold and bacteria. Usually, these bacteria are harmless or aren't concentrated enough to make you sick; however, other diseases could be lurking. If you don't wipe off the top, the tab will transfer bacteria into the drink when it plunges into the liquid upon opening the can. Sipping from a straw through a clean spout will keep you safe from anything that may be living on the surface of the can.

⚠ *WORDS OF CAUTION: There is a remote (but real) possibility that you could catch hantavirus, an often fatal respiratory pathogen spread by rodents, from the top of a soda can. This could happen if the cans were kept outside or in a garage and were exposed to rat or mouse droppings.*

WHAT IS THE SAFEST AMOUNT OF CAFFEINE TO ALLOW IN YOUR DIET?

250 MG A DAY (ABOUT TWO CUPS OF COFFEE OR SIX CUPS OF TEA) OR LESS.

WHY? Sure, it helps you stay awake at 4 A.M., but most doctors will tell you that caffeine is just not good for you. But it's not terrible for you either, as long as you don't overdo it. A few cups of coffee or tea a day have not been linked with any serious health risks for most adults.

⚠ *WORDS OF CAUTION: While it may not kill you, ingesting a lot of caffeine does have some adverse health effects, including increased heart rate, nausea, irritability, stress, and insomnia. But remember: Coffee's not the only culprit. Caffeine can also be found in chocolate, colas, various over-the-counter painkillers (which sometimes have more caffeine than a cup of coffee), appetite suppressants, and cold medicines.*

Approximate Caffeine Content in Popular Products

Brewed coffee (5 oz/150 ml)	115 mg
Instant coffee (5 oz/150 ml)	65 mg
Decaf coffee, brewed (5 oz/150 ml)	3 mg
Decaf coffee, instant (5 oz/150ml)	2 mg
Espresso (3 oz/90 ml)	100 mg
Brewed tea (5 oz/150 ml)	40 mg
Instant tea (5 oz/150 ml)	30 mg
Iced tea (12 oz/350 ml glass)	45 mg
Soda (6 oz/180 ml)	18 mg
Hot chocolate (5 oz/150 ml)	4 mg
Dark chocolate (30 g)	20 mg
Headache medicine (2 tablets)	130 mg

WHAT IS THE SAFEST ARTIFICIAL SWEETENER?

SUCRALOSE.

WHY? Sucralose, manufactured in the U.S. as Splenda®, is a derivative of sucrose (table sugar) that has more than 300 times the sweetness of regular sugar. Because it is not absorbed by the digestive tract, it has no calories. It's considered safer than other sweeteners because it's made from sugar, unlike others, which are made from combinations of amino acids and chemicals.

⚠ *WORDS OF CAUTION: Avoid saccharin. While there has been no concrete evidence that it causes cancer, there is no evidence to exclude that possibility. Though the U.S. Food and Drug Administration (FDA) says saccharin is safe, some studies have linked it to bladder cancer when consumed in large quantities.*

There has been much debate over the safety of saccharin's rival NutraSweet® (also known as Equal®). Some studies have suggested it causes brain tumors, while others have said it triggers migraines. The FDA, however, stands by the sweetener, saying it poses no health risk except for people with phenylketonuria, a rare, inherited metabolic condition.

CHILLED AND HELD AT A 45-DEGREE ANGLE, WITH A TOWEL ON TOP.

WHY? You don't want your midnight toast to end up in a black—or blind—eye. Bad technique and a warm bottle can result in serious eye injuries and painful bruising. The cork of a warm bottle is more likely to pop unexpectedly, so chilling your bubbly will do more than just improve the taste.

The Perfect Technique

1. Hold the cork down with the palm of your hand while you untwist and remove the wire hood.

2. Point the bottle away from yourself and others.

3. Place a towel over the top to catch the cork when it pops out.

4. Tilt the bottle at a 45-degree angle (so the cork shoots toward the ceiling, not your friends).

5. Slowly and firmly twist the cork to break the seal.

6. Maintaining a 45-degree angle, hold the bottle firmly with one hand and use the other to slowly turn the cork with a slight upward pull.

7. Steadily twist and pull until the cork is almost out of the neck.

8. As the cork breaks free from the bottle, apply a slight downward pressure to stop the cork from shooting forward.

NOTE: *There is no need to be dramatic when popping the champagne. Easing off the cork saves the bubbles and air from being lost. Let it slide out slowly.*

CHAPTER 4

IN THE BATHROOM

WHAT IS THE SAFEST WAY TO BATHE?

IN A STALL SHOWER WITH A SLIP-RESISTANT FLOOR AND LOW-TO-THE-GROUND EDGES.

WHY? More than 100,000 people suffer bathtub- or shower-related injuries every year. Bathtubs are the greatest hazard; as many as 500 people a year die getting in or out of the tub. The wet, slick surfaces make for hazardous footing, which can be easily counteracted by a non-stick mat or other slip-resistant treatment. Additionally, stepping over the edge of the tub can put you in a precarious position, leading to a fall; a stall-type shower with low edges avoids this problem altogether.

⚠ *WORDS OF CAUTION:* *Putting a bathmat next to the shower does more than just keep your feet from getting the tile wet after your shower. A towel or slip-resistant rug can keep you from slipping on your wet feet as you step out.*

WHAT IS THE SAFEST WAY TO WASH YOUR HANDS?

USING AN ANTIBACTERIAL SOAP OR GEL.

WHY? Every day, your hands are exposed to millions of germs, causing anything from the common cold and flu to hepatitis and herpes. You could use regular soap and water to wash your hands—but most people don't give themselves the necessary 20 to 30 seconds of vigorous scrubbing to rid their skin of germs. An antibacterial soap will do some of the work for you. If soap is unavailable, use an alcohol-based antibacterial gel, which will kill germs, viruses, and bacteria living on your skin without the need for soap and water.

⚠ *WORDS OF CAUTION: Some scientists believe that use of antibacterial products may weaken the body's natural germ-fighting ability. Microbiologists disagree, saying no antibacterial product has been proven to do so. In fact, antibacterial products were developed for use in hospitals to keep doctors and nurses from carrying germs on their hands.*

WHAT IS THE SAFEST PLACE TO STORE YOUR TOOTHBRUSH?

IN THE MEDICINE CABINET.

WHY? Every time you flush the toilet, millions of bacteria are propelled into the air. Storing your toothbrush in the open practically invites germs to land on those damp, bacteria-friendly bristles. Your medicine cabinet, by contrast, keeps your brush safe from flying germs.

⚠ *WORDS OF CAUTION: Don't store your toothbrush in a covered toothbrush holder. Bacteria love darkness and will flourish in the extremely small, lightless, humid environment of a covered holder. Store your toothbrush in an upright position (e.g., standing in a cup) to allow it to fully dry.*

WHAT IS THE SAFEST NUMBER OF TIMES TO USE A DISPOSABLE RAZOR?

THREE.

WHY? Not all razor blades are created equal. Disposable razors are thinner than other razors and therefore more prone to nicking your skin and producing microscopic cuts. The longer you keep a razor, the more germs can collect, which could leave you with a bacterial infection.

⚠ *WORDS OF CAUTION:* *Never share razors. You risk exposure to a whole host of pathogens that may enter small cuts or broken skin. Hepatitis and herpes are just two of many illnesses you could contract.*

Those little red bumps that sometimes appear after shaving may indicate folliculitis, tiny infections inside the hair follicle that can be caused by a razor past its prime. If the condition worsens or persists for several weeks, see your doctor.

Do not store your razor in the shower, where the moist environment allows for the rapid growth of bacteria.

WHAT IS THE SAFEST WAY TO COLOR YOUR HAIR?

WITH HENNA-BASED DYES.

WHY? Henna is a vegetable dye and is less harmful because it does not contain the potentially danger-ous chemicals found in permanent dyes such as ammonia or bleach. Semipermanent and tempo-rary chemical dyes are also thought by experts to be safer than permanent dyes.

⚠ *WORDS OF CAUTION: If you're looking to change your hair color to something other than the red that henna produces, do so only in moderation. While experts maintain the health risks posed by chemical hair dyes are minimal, several studies have shown a remote link between the chemicals in the dyes and different types of cancer. A study by the American Cancer Institute in the 1990s found that women who used black permanent dye for 20 years or more had an increased risk of dying of non-Hodgkin's lymphoma and multiple myeloma, both cancers of the immune system. Additionally, a study published in the* International Journal of Cancer *found that women who use permanent hair dyes at least once a month for a year or longer have twice the risk of developing bladder cancer as non-users, as do colorists who apply the dyes.*

CHAPTER 5

MAN'S BEST FRIEND

WHAT IS THE SAFEST WAY TO MEET A DOG?

MAKE A RELAXED FIST, LET THE DOG SMELL THE BACK OF YOUR HAND, THEN PET ITS SHOULDERS OR CHEST.

WHY? Dogs often bite because they're fearful. Giving a dog (even your own) the opportunity to see and smell you before you pet him can put him at ease. Keeping your hand in a fist ensures that you won't lose a finger if the dog changes his mind. When you put your hand out, don't stick it right into the dog's face; rather, hold it out and let the dog come toward you. Once the gesture is accepted, pet the dog on the shoulders or the chest. These areas are less sensitive, and the dog is less likely to perceive the petting as a threat.

⚠ **WORDS OF CAUTION:** *Never pet a strange dog on the top of the head. In the wild, when two dogs (or wolves) meet each other for the first time, one may establish dominance by putting a paw over the other dog's neck. When you reach toward a dog's head, the dog may think you're offering a challenge and may react. Also, do* *not make direct eye contact, which can be threatening; instead, look briefly at the dog, then look away. This tells the dog you are not challenging it.*

One of the first signs a dog is going to bite is tension. If you notice the dog is tensing up as you pet him, pull your hand away. Dogs are also more likely to bite if you disturb them while they're sleeping, eating, chewing on a toy, or caring for puppies. Be extra careful around pit bulls, rottweilers, German shepherds, huskies, chows, and akitas: They're the breeds most often involved in deadly attacks.

WHAT IS THE SAFEST KIND OF OVER-THE-COUNTER PAIN RELIEVER TO GIVE A DOG?

BUFFERED ASPIRIN.

WHY? While it's not completely hazard free, buffered aspirin is the painkiller most often recommended by veterinarians. Just be careful with the dosage: Too much—even a few doses—can give your pooch stomach problems and ulcers. Use one-quarter of a 325-mg tablet for every 10 pounds (4.5 kg) your dog weighs.

⚠ *WORDS OF CAUTION: Do not give your dog any product containing acetaminophen or ibuprofen; these medicines can be deadly to dogs. (Don't ever give cats human painkillers; even small doses can kill them.) It's always best to consult your vet before you start popping pills into your pet, since even the "safest" medications can be dangerous if not administered carefully.*

WHAT IS THE SAFEST WAY TO TRANSPORT A PET?

BY CAR.

WHY? Cars, unlike planes, do not experience temperature fluctuations or air pressure changes, and are generally less noisy, scary environments for your pet. You can also monitor your pet's condition more carefully in a car.

Make sure your pet is secure. Dogs should be restrained, either by crate or with a harness that attaches to a seat belt, to keep them from climbing over the seats, distracting the driver, and jumping out the moment the door is opened.

Cats are safest in a crate, where they can feel secure and won't end up under the seats or beneath the driver's feet. The crate should be large enough to allow your pet to sit, stand, and change position comfortably. Attach the crate to a seat belt to prevent slipping.

The best mode of travel for a seeing-eye dog is

flying, since all U.S. airlines must allow service animals in the cabin. They don't have to be in a carrier, but they must be harnessed.

⚠ **WORDS OF CAUTION:** *Don't let your dog stick his head out the window while driving. The wind can hurl particles of dirt into his eyes, ears, and nose, which can lead to injury or infection, not to mention the risk of another car coming too close. Large amounts of cold air in your dog's lungs can cause illness.*

Avoid flying with your pet if you must transport your pet in the cargo or baggage holds in the belly of the plane. According to the American Society for the Prevention of Cruelty to Animals (ASPCA), about 5,000 animals are lost, injured, or killed each year while being transported as cargo or baggage. (This is approximately 1 percent of the half a million pets that fly each year in the United States.) If you must fly with your pet, get a nonstop flight; they're the safest (page 88), and you don't want to find out your "baggage" didn't make the connection. Keep in mind that while baggage compartments are supposed to be pressurized and heated, if something goes wrong, your pet is only considered "damaged baggage." You can't sue.

CHAPTER 6

SPORTS AND
ENTERTAINMENT

WHAT IS THE SAFEST SPECTATOR PROFESSIONAL SPORT?

TENNIS.

WHY? Tennis equipment rarely malfunctions, and tennis spectators rarely become combative (especially compared with football fans). There has never been a fatality from an errant tennis ball at a major tennis event. And although the Professional Golfers Association of America (PGA) maintains that nobody has ever been killed by a flying golf ball, either, it's not uncommon for spectators or even players to be struck during that sport.

⚠ **WORDS OF CAUTION:** *Stray balls or pucks are not all you have to worry about at sporting events. Spectators sitting in bleachers can fall; fans sitting in the hot sun can get heatstroke or suffer from dehydration; and whenever large groups of people are confined together in a closed space, you face the risk of danger from pushing and shoving matches to stampedes and riots.*

WHAT IS THE SAFEST SEAT AT A MAJOR-LEAGUE BASEBALL GAME?

DIRECTLY BEHIND THE BACKSTOP, UNDER THE PROTECTIVE SCREEN.

WHY? Major-League baseball stadiums provide netting to protect spectators from foul balls that speed toward the area behind the batter. Alternatively, choose a seat in the upper decks of the stadium; it's so far away from the batter, a batted ball is unlikely to reach you (and if it does, at least you'll have a lot of time to get away—or make the catch).

⚠ *WORDS OF CAUTION:* *The protective screen isn't fully enclosed, so watch out if you are seated right outside the safety net. You may want to catch a foul ball, but not with your face. Those balls are heading at you at about 80 mph (129 km/h). Line-drive foul balls are also prone to shoot out along the first- and third-base lines and could be deadly. Players have also been known to lose grip of their bats, which occasionally fly into the stands on the third- or first-base sides. The barrels of shattered bats also find their way into the seats.*

WHAT IS THE SAFEST SEAT AT A PROFESSIONAL HOCKEY GAME?

BEHIND THE GOAL, AT LEAST FOUR ROWS UP.

WHY? Pucks reportedly shoot into the stands in the U.S. an average of 12 times per game (though fewer than five people have ever been fatally injured). To protect fans, National Hockey League arenas are required to have at least a 5-foot (1.5 m) tall Plexiglas barrier surrounding the ice and a 68-foot (21 m) tall nylon mesh netting behind each goal, where most errant pucks fly. Plexiglas can break, so don't sit right behind it. Instead, sit a few rows up, where you're protected by the net. If you can't get these seats, head up to the highest rows, where even the most errant pucks can't reach.

⚠ **WORDS OF CAUTION:** *The players' pre-game 15-minute warm-up is considered the most dangerous time to be in a hockey arena; most fans are are not paying attention, and there are dozens of players and lots of pucks on the ice.*

ON THE STRAIGHTAWAY, IN THE LAST ROW (ON AN OVAL TRACK).

WHY? If a racecar is going to crash, it will likely happen as it goes around the bend. Sitting in the middle of the straightaway, in a row far from the track, you're least likely to be struck by any debris.

⚠ ***WORDS OF CAUTION:*** *Bear in mind that auto races are some of the most dangerous sporting events. Always pay attention to your surroundings as you move around the stadium. According to a report compiled by the Charlotte Observer, more than 29 spectators have been killed and more than 70 injured since 1990 at car and truck races after car parts—including broken glass, sheets of metal, and tires—shot into the stands. This is greater than that of all other professional sports, which each average fewer than three equipment-related deaths in history.*

WHAT IS THE SAFEST PIECE OF GYM EQUIPMENT?

THE ELLIPTICAL MACHINE.

WHY? Not only is the elliptical machine better on your joints than other cardiovascular machines, but it also has a lower injury rate than other cardio machines, including stair steppers and stationary bikes.

⚠ **WORDS OF CAUTION:** *Be careful on the treadmill. According to health and fitness experts, treadmills are second only to free weights in causing gym-equipment-related injuries in the U.S. Most of the time, these injuries occur when people get on or off the treadmill improperly or lose their balance while running.*

WHAT IS THE SAFEST SEAT AT A CONCERT?

A RESERVED SEAT NEAR AN EXIT.

WHY? In one U.S. study of nearly 250 concerts, 90 percent of the more than 22,000 concert injuries occurred in or near unreserved (i.e., general admission) or standing-room-only areas. If you're sitting near an exit—or you are aware of where the exits are—you'll have an easier time getting out in the event of an emergency.

Standing-room-only areas and general admission seating are far and away the most dangerous locales because they have the least amount of crowd management; fans tend to get rowdier, often pushing toward the front of the stage. Always avoid the mosh pit.

⚠ *WORDS OF CAUTION: Choose your concerts wisely. Studies have shown that rap concerts are the most violent and rock concerts (including heavy metal) the most reckless. Folk and country shows and, not surprisingly, classical music and opera have few reported problems.*

WHAT IS THE SAFEST KIND OF FIREWORKS?

A SPARKLER (AS LONG AS YOU'RE NOT HOLDING IT IN YOUR HANDS).

WHY? If you're going to set off fireworks (which safety experts caution against), use small ones such as sparklers or fountains that don't "explode" or shoot out into the air. The potential for injuries is less severe. But keep in mind that sparklers burn at up to 1,800°F (982°C). If you hold one in your hands you risk burning yourself or setting your clothes on fire. Instead, set the sparkler in a pot of sand or another non-flammable container.

⚠ **WORDS OF CAUTION:** *According to the Centers for Disease Control and Prevention, an estimated 9,500 people are injured in the U.S. each year while either orchestrating or watching home-made fireworks displays.*

Homemade and illegal fireworks, bottle rockets, firecrackers, and sparklers are the biggest causes of fire-works-related injuries. Bottle rockets, illegal in many states, are the most likely to cause eye injuries, since they can shoot out unpredictably and can exceed temperatures of more than 1,000°F (538°C).

WHAT IS THE SAFEST AMUSEMENT PARK RIDE?

THE FERRIS WHEEL.

WHY? In a study of popular amusement rides—including roller coasters, whirling rides, water slides, and trains—Ferris wheels were ranked the safest, with only two deaths in a 13-year period. With a Ferris wheel's slow-moving parts and enclosed cabs, you're not likely to fall, get sick, or otherwise be injured.

⚠ *WORDS OF CAUTION: While it is still extremely rare (the odds of being killed on an amusement park ride are about 1 in 760 million), roller coasters account for the highest number of ride fatalities, with an average of one death per year in the U.S. Minor injuries, such as cuts and bruises, aren't as rare: Statistics show an average of 10,000 people per year (out of 1.5 billion riders) suffer minor injuries. Roller coasters are the hardest on your body, with neck sprains the most commonly reported injury. To be safe, keep your head against the headrest and face straight ahead during a roller coaster ride.*

WHAT IS THE SAFEST PIECE OF PLAYGROUND EQUIPMENT?

A SPRING-LOADED SEESAW.

WHY? Falling is the most common cause of playground injury, making swinging and climbing the most dangerous playground activities. More than 200,000 preschool and elementary school kids go to emergency rooms after getting hurt on playgrounds, according to the Centers for Disease Control and Prevention. About 70 percent of these injuries are caused by falls. Shorter, secured, slow moving or stationary equipment, such as a seesaw, is safest.

⚠ **WORDS OF CAUTION:** *Always supervise children as they climb on a jungle gym. Do not let them climb on anything unless there's a soft ground surface below them, such as shredded rubber, wood chips, or sand. Older playgrounds built on pavement pose particular dangers.*

CHAPTER 7

TRAVEL AND THE GREAT OUTDOORS

WHAT IS THE SAFEST KIND OF HOTEL?

ONE NEAR THE AIRPORT.

WHY? A Cornell University study found that hotels near U.S. airports generally offer more safety and security features, including sprinklers and security cameras, than those found closer to towns and cities. This may be because they play host to more business travelers who are accustomed to (and might demand) such amenities. In addition, hotels near airports usually are newer and therefore adhere to more modern standards for safety.

⚠ *WORDS OF CAUTION:* *Be careful of motels with no interior hallways. Such layouts allow anyone outside to see what room you're in and when you're leaving it. If you can't go elsewhere, take a room that does not face the parking lot so that others can't see your comings and goings.*

WHAT IS THE SAFEST ROOM IN A HOTEL?

NEAR THE ELEVATOR, BETWEEN THE FOURTH AND SEVENTH FLOORS.

WHY? Rooms near elevators, while noisier, are generally safer because they have more foot traffic. Rooms between the fourth and seventh floor are high enough to dissuade intruders attempting to enter through a window but are still reachable by fire ladder if you need to be evacuated. (Most fire ladders don't reach more than seven stories.)

⚠ *WORDS OF CAUTION: Never take a room above the seventh floor. Not only will firefighters have a harder time reaching you, but it'll be tougher to evacuate if you have to navigate possibly smoky stairwells. Avoid staying on the first floor; it's the most likely break-in location. If you have to stay on the ground level, ask for a room that faces an inside courtyard instead of the parking lot.*

WHAT IS THE SAFEST WAY TO SLEEP IN A MOTEL BED?

WITH THE BEDSPREAD OFF.

WHY? *E. coli*, semen, urine, yeast, mold, lice, and bedbugs are among the things you might find lurking in your hotel room. Reports have shown that while most motels and hotels wash the sheets and pillowcases between guests, the bedspreads are often left for long periods without being washed. You're probably not likely to get seriously sick, but the things lurking below the surface are pretty disturbing. The American Automobile Association (AAA) recommends taking the cover off the bed before sleeping and putting a towel on any stained or dirty surfaces before sitting down.

⚠ **WORDS OF CAUTION:** *If the room seems particularly dirty, be on the lookout for bedbugs, which are small insects that live in bedding, furniture, and walls. Rooms with a bedbug infestation are said to have a musty, sweet odor. You may also want to clean both the hotel remote control and the phone with a disinfectant wipe; tests done by AAA have found that they may harbor bacteria, germs, or bodily fluids.*

WHAT IS THE SAFEST PLACE TO PITCH A TENT?

BESIDE LOW BUSHES.

WHY? Two of the greatest dangers when camping are lightning strikes and falling branches. Camping next to low-lying (that is, lower than your tent) bushes can protect you from the wind but will not leave you vulnerable to falling objects.

⚠ *WORDS OF CAUTION: Never camp in dry riverbeds; these areas are prone to flash floods. When you pitch your tent, make sure it's at least 50 yards (45.5 meters) away from your kitchen area so that you don't run into any bears looking for food. It's also best if you're upwind from the eating area, since bears are known to be attracted by even the faintest smell of food. (Obviously, don't keep any food inside your tent.) Some campsites provide bear-proof boxes for your food—use them. If no boxes are available, bag your food items in airtight bags and hang them from a tree or cable at least 10 feet (3 meters) above the ground and 4 feet (1.2 meters) out from any vertical support.*

WEARING DULL, NON-CONTRASTING COLORS DURING DAYLIGHT HOURS.

WHY? Sharks can see contrast well, and bright colors seem to attract them. To be safe, dull-colored bathing suits with no clear contrasts should be worn. Especially avoid black and white stripes, which can be seen particularly well by sharks.

⚠ *WORDS OF CAUTION: Take off any shiny jewelry before going in the water. To a shark, jewels and silver may resemble the sheen of fish scales. Also, be careful in the area between sandbars or near steep dropoffs; these are favorite hangouts for sharks. The hours between dusk and dawn are treacherous, too. If it's dark out, don't swim. And don't enter the water if you are bleeding from an open wound or if you are menstruating—sharks may be attracted by the scent of blood.*

WHAT IS THE SAFEST CITY IN THE UNITED STATES?

AMHERST, NEW YORK.

WHY? According to the most recent Morgan Quitno survey, which compares FBI crime data of 342 major cities nationwide (all with more than 75,000 people), Amherst had the lowest combined rate of murder, rape, robbery, aggravated assault, burglary, and motor vehicle theft per capita. Annually in Amherst there are only about 30 robberies, no murders, and only about 100 car thefts.

Amherst Chief of Police John Moslow credited its "safest city" status to its suburban setting and affluent, well-educated population (it's a suburb of Buffalo and near the University of Buffalo), but said that the low crime rates are also due to the ample resources provided to the police department by the town board year after year. Considering that other suburban areas with similar population and demographics have higher crime rates, the Amherst PD must be doing something right.

As for the nation's largest cities—those with 500,000 people or more—San Jose, California; Honolulu, Hawaii; and El Paso, Texas, rank as the safest. (Note: The survey, which is based on 2001 FBI statistics, did not include Chicago, San Francisco, or Alexandria, Virginia; crime information submitted by these cities was either incomplete or inconsistent with FBI criteria.)

⚠ **WORDS OF CAUTION:** *The Gateway to the West may not be such a safe meeting place. According to the most recent survey, St. Louis, which fits in the same population grouping as Amherst (100,000 to 500,000 people), ranked highest in overall U.S. crime rates, with about 125 murders, 3,000 robberies, and 9,000 car thefts per year. Detroit and Atlanta were the next most perilous.*

WHAT IS THE SAFEST CITY FOR AIR QUALITY IN THE UNITED STATES?

BELLINGHAM, WASHINGTON.

WHY? According to the American Lung Association, the city of Bellingham, Washington, far from any metropolis, has the least amount of ozone air pollution, followed by Sioux Falls, South Dakota. Ozone, an ingredient in smog and a major cause of lung disease, is created when sunlight acts on chemicals created by fuel combustion. When you breathe polluted air, ozone in your lungs can inflame and irritate your respiratory system.

⚠ **WORDS OF CAUTION:** *California—and not just the smoggy Hollywood Hills—has the highest levels of ozone pollution in the country. The Los Angeles metropolitan area consistently ranks as the most polluted city in the country (according to the American Lung Association), with Bakersfield, Fresno, and Visalia-Tulare-Porterville, also in California, next in line.*

WHAT IS THE SAFEST PLACE WHEN OUTDOORS DURING A LIGHTNING STORM?

IN A CAR WITH A METAL ROOF.

WHY? About 400 people are struck by lightning each year in the U.S., according to the National Weather Service. Cars are safe havens because lightning currents travel over the outside of cars rather than through them. Contrary to popular opinion, car tires don't "absorb" the electric shock of a lightning strike—it's the cage of metal around you that protects you.

⚠ ***WORDS OF CAUTION:*** *If you can't get to a car or other shelter, it's best to put away any metal items (such as golf clubs and umbrellas) and get yourself to a low-lying area. If there are no low areas, crouch close to the ground until the storm passes. Whatever you do, make sure that you're not the tallest thing around; you'd be a more attractive target. And remember: If you can hear thunder, you are within lightning striking distance.*

WHERE IS THE SAFEST PLACE WHEN INDOORS DURING A LIGHTNING STORM?

INTERIOR ROOMS, AWAY FROM ELECTRICAL APPLIANCES.

WHY? When lightning strikes a house, it can travel through the outer walls and gutters or through wiring and plumbing, which generally run from the outside of the house. If you're in an interior room, you're typically farther away from these hazards.

⚠ *WORDS OF CAUTION:* *Avoid talking on corded phones during a lightning storm; lightning can travel through standard phone cords (cordless phones and cell phones are okay, though; see page 16). Avoid contact with plumbing. Do not wash your hands, take a shower, wash dishes, or do the laundry until the storm has passed.*

WHAT IS THE SAFEST PLACE TO BE DURING A TORNADO?

IN A BASEMENT.

WHY? Flying debris and shattered glass cause the highest number of deaths and injuries during a tornado. Basements are generally lacking in windows and are below the level at which the tornado is traveling. If you don't have a basement, go to a windowless interior room on the lowest floor. This could be a hallway, a bathroom, or a closet. Once you're there, get underneath something sturdy such as a heavy table and cover yourself with a blanket, sleeping bag, or mattress to add a layer of protection from any flying debris if possible.

If you're on the road, get out of your car, but don't try to outrun the twister. Cars and trucks are easily tossed by tornados. Instead, find a low-lying area, cover your head with your hands, and lie there until the tornado passes. Don't hide beneath cars or near trees, both of which could end up being slammed down on top of you if the tornado picks them up.

Tornado Warning Signs

• The "calm before the storm." Right before a tornado hits, the wind may die down, and the air may become very still.

• A moving cloud of debris. The funnel may be in the center of this cloud.

• A dark or green-colored sky.

• Large hail.

⚠ **WORDS OF CAUTION:** *Contrary to popular belief, the space under an overpass is not safe during a tornado. Twister winds pick up debris at up to 200 mph (320 km/h); overpasses tend to be collection areas for this debris.*

Know the difference between a "tornado watch" and a "tornado warning." A "watch" is issued when weather conditions are favorable for tornados; be alert and tune into local radio or TV stations for more information. A "warning" is issued when a tornado has been sighted or spotted on weather radar; take shelter immediately.

WHAT IS THE SAFEST PLACE TO BE DURING A HURRICANE?

AN INTERIOR ROOM OF A (NON-MOBILE) HOME ON THE FIRST OR SECOND FLOOR.

WHY? As with a tornado, flying debris and broken glass are the most immediate threats during a hurricane. Boarding up all the windows and skylights and staying in the inner rooms of a home will keep you safe from the storm's high winds.

A hurricane's real damage is usually done in the form of flooding and power outages. Do not stay in the basement, the most likely place to flood.

⚠ *WORDS OF CAUTION: Hurricanes are the most damaging in coastal areas, where the water can surge up to 25 feet (7.6 m) above normal high tide. If you live on the beach or near a river or lake, be prepared to travel at least 20 miles (32 km) inland, where the damage and flooding will be less severe.*

To prepare, stock up on flashlights, a week's worth of bottled water, food, a non-electric can opener, and basic first-aid supplies. Have fresh batteries to power a battery-operated radio for listening to emergency broadcasts.

CHAPTER 8

PLANES, TRAINS, AND
AUTOMOBILES

WHAT IS THE SAFEST KIND OF FLIGHT TO TAKE?

A NONSTOP FLIGHT.

WHY? Most airplane crashes happen during takeoff and landing. Limiting the number of takeoffs and landings helps increase your chances of avoiding an accident.

⚠ **WORDS OF CAUTION:** *Airplane accident rates are unrelated to length of time in the air; you could be on a five-hour flight from Los Angeles to New York or a 20-minute jump from Austin to Houston—your chances of being in an accident, provided you are on the same type of airplane, are the same. Note that booking a "nonstop" flight means that there are no stops, but that a "direct" flight might include a stopover on the way—therefore, "direct" flights are not necessarily safer options.*

A LARGE-SIZED (MORE THAN 30-SEAT) COMMERCIAL JET AIRLINE.

WHY? According to the Federal Aviation Administration (FAA), studies have shown that major U.S. domestic carriers using jet aircraft (as opposed to turboprop planes) have lower accident rates than smaller U.S. regional or commuter carriers. This is largely because in addition to being designed under stricter standards, larger aircraft (those with more than 30 seats) are heavier and therefore more durable in the face of impact and turbulence. Commercial airlines are also more carefully maintained.

⚠ *WORDS OF CAUTION: Avoid small planes. Statistics show you're three times more likely to die in a crash on a plane with 30 or fewer seats. Smaller planes often use regional airports that may not be well equipped to guide planes at night. Studies have also shown, not surprisingly, that airlines based in the U.S. and other developed countries have consistently fewer accidents than airlines based in less-developed countries.*

WHAT IS THE SAFEST LOCATION ON A PLANE?

IN A WINDOW SEAT NEAR THE WING.

WHY? About 70 percent of the people who die in survivable plane crashes reportedly die of smoke inhalation after the plane has come to a stop. At that point, smoke and fire are the greatest dangers. You're safest if you're sitting near the wing, which is the strongest part of the plane and likely to be close to the emergency exits.

⚠ ***WORDS OF CAUTION:*** *Crash worries aside, you might want to choose a window seat at the front of the plane if you're concerned about falling objects or motion sickness. A window seat will help you avoid being struck by items falling from the overhead storage bins. (Statistics report that overhead bin accidents account for about 4,500 injuries in the U.S. each year). Meanwhile, the back of the plane whips around the most in turbulence. No matter what seat you're in, stand up and stretch your legs every few hours, and take an aspirin before flying to thin your blood. Sitting for longer than five hours increases your chances of getting a blood clot in your legs known as a thrombus.*

WHAT IS THE SAFEST FORM OF MASS TRANSIT?

LIGHT RAIL (TROLLEYS).

WHY? According to Department of Transportation statistics, there are fewer fatalities and injuries as well as fewer crimes on light rail systems than on trains or buses.

⚠ *WORDS OF CAUTION:* *Be careful when riding a bus. At about 40,000 injuries in the United States per year, more people are hurt riding buses than any other form of transit; most of these are minor slips and falls. Heavy rail ranks as most dangerous for crime, with more than 2,000 robberies and 6,000 thefts per year on intercity trains in the U.S. (see page 92).*

WHAT IS THE SAFEST CAR ON A TRAIN?

THE FRONT OR MIDDLE CAR, WHICH-EVER IS CLOSEST TO THE CONDUCTOR OR CONDUCTOR'S ASSISTANT.

WHY? Train wrecks are rare; train crime is common-place. There are a handful of fatal train accidents per year, but the U.S. Department of Transportation reports an average of 2,000 robberies and 1,000 aggravated assaults on heavy rail trains annually. Transit officials advise passengers—especially when traveling at night or when the train is not full—to choose a seat near the conductor (there is usually one at the front of the train and an assistant in the middle). That way, there's someone nearby who can call for help if you're in trouble.

⚠ *WORDS OF CAUTION: Never sit in the last car on the train when traveling at night. This car is more likely to be empty, and it leaves you at risk for being cornered.*

WHAT IS THE SAFEST TYPE OF CAR TO DRIVE?

A LARGE, FOUR-DOOR CAR.

WHY? Large vehicles usually have longer crumple zones, preventing damage to the area surrounding the occupants. According to statistics, very large cars, or cars weighing more than 3,000 pounds (1,360 kg) with wheelbases longer than 115 inches (292 cm) and lengths longer than 210 inches (533 cm), are least likely to be involved in deadly wrecks.

⚠ **WORDS OF CAUTION:** *Heavy SUVs and vans are also safe in multiple-vehicle crashes, but their weight benefits are overshadowed by their propensity for rollovers. According to the American Insurance Institute for Highway Safety (IIHS), nearly 80 percent of deaths in single-vehicle crashes of SUVs involve rollovers, compared with 62 percent for pickups and 48 percent for cars.*

Very small cars are also dangerous, with the highest number of crash fatalities of any vehicle type at about 16 fatalities per billion miles driven; that's compared to only 7 fatalities per billion miles traveled in large cars, 9 fatalities per billion miles traveled in midsize cars, and 10 fatalities per billion miles traveled in large SUVs.

WHAT IS THE SAFEST SEAT IN A CAR?

THE BACKSEAT.

WHY? According to data from the U.S. Department of Transportation, rear-impact crashes make up only about 5 percent of vehicle-occupant fatalities. Statistics show that most accidents are head-on, with the right and left sides being hit with equal frequency. If you're in the backseat, you're likely to be the farthest away from the point of impact.

⚠ **WORDS OF CAUTION:** *Think twice before calling shotgun. Frontal impacts account for about 50 percent of all vehicle-occupant deaths. In addition, never put small children in a passenger seat with an airbag; the bag may pop out and suffocate or injure them. All children under 12 should ride in the backseat, and every U.S. state has child restraint laws requiring children to be in approved safety seats. According to the National Highway Traffic Safety Administration, babies and toddlers should always ride in car seats designed for their weight/height group.*

THE MIDDLE LANE.

WHY? According to experts at the American Automobile Association (AAA), the middle lane is safest because it saves you from potential conflicts with merging or exiting traffic and still leaves the left lane to pass and be passed.

⚠ *WORDS OF CAUTION: Avoid driving in the right lane, where you have to watch out for a slew of potential hazards, including merging traffic, car doors opening, stalled vehicles, cyclists, pedestrians, and animals. In the left lane, stay alert for oncoming cars swerving out of their lanes.*

WHAT IS THE SAFEST DAY OF THE WEEK TO GO FOR A DRIVE?

MONDAY OR TUESDAY.

WHY? According to the Department of Transportation, the least number of fatal accidents occur on Mondays and Tuesdays, probably because that's when the fewest number of people are out on the road (there's just more going on over the weekend and toward the end of the week).

⚠ **WORDS OF CAUTION:** *Be extra careful driving on Saturdays and Sundays. Statistics show that accidents dramatically increase over the weekends, because more people are likely out on the road.*

WHAT IS THE SAFEST COLOR CAR TO DRIVE?

LIME GREEN.

WHY? Studies have shown that lime green is the most visible color on the road. Don't want a car that glows? Yellow is the next best easy-to-see car color.

⚠ *WORDS OF CAUTION:* *Black cars are about 10 times as hard to see as lighter color cars—especially at night—and consequently are involved in more accidents. Red cars, which appear black at night, are also hard to see.*

WHAT IS THE SAFEST PLACE TO PULL OVER WHEN STOPPED BY AN UNMARKED POLICE CAR?

A WELL-LIT PUBLIC LOCATION (IF NEARBY).

WHY? It's against the law to continue driving after you've been ordered by a police officer to pull over. That said, if there's a well-lit area (such as a gas station or public parking lot) within a quarter mile of where you've been asked to stop, it is safest to pull over there. Put on your hazard lights to indicate you've seen the officer, and drive to that location. At that point, you have the right to keep your windows rolled up and ask to see a badge. You can also legally demand (through a cracked or unopened window) that the officer call a marked car for backup.

⚠ *WORDS OF CAUTION:* *If you have a cell phone, call 911 (contrary to urban legend, #77 doesn't work in all states), report your location, and make sure the police officer following you is for real.*

WHAT IS THE SAFEST PLACE TO PARK IN A PARKING GARAGE?

ON THE GROUND FLOOR, NEAR THE ATTENDANT.

WHY? Parking garages rank third among top locations for violent crime (after homes and public streets). To lessen your chances of being attacked, park on the street level near the attendant. The attendant's presence will deter criminals, and he or she can call for help if you need assistance. Additionally, parking on the ground floor means you won't have to use the stairs or elevator (both targets for lurking criminals) to get in and out.

⚠ **WORDS OF CAUTION:** *Be extra careful when taking the elevator or stairs in parking garages. Studies have shown they're the most dangerous spots in a garage. Because fire codes have dictated that they be enclosed, they offer criminals a wealth of hiding spots. Also be sure to avoid parking next to large trucks, vans, or Dumpsters, which provide handy hiding places for attackers.*

WHAT IS THE SAFEST STATE TO DRIVE IN?

MASSACHUSETTS.

WHY? According to studies, the Northeast is generally safer for driving because the speed limits are lower and the roads are more congested. Massachusetts has been ranked as the safest, with only 0.8 deaths per 100 million miles (160 million km) traveled in a recent year, compared to a national average of 1.5 deaths. Connecticut, New Jersey, and Rhode Island are also reported to be safe places for a drive.

⚠ *WORDS OF CAUTION:* *It may be fun to drive on those endless desert highways, but be careful. According to the American Automobile Association (AAA), Western states, including Montana, Wyoming, and Arizona, are the most dangerous for drivers, with about 2.2 deaths per 100 million miles (160 million km) traveled. Experts say that wide-open spaces combined with higher speed limits and fewer hospitals translate into a higher incidence of traffic fatalities.*

CHAPTER 9

EVERYDAY SAFETY

WHAT IS THE SAFEST TIME TO GO TO THE BANK?

TUESDAY THROUGH THURSDAY, BETWEEN 3 P.M. AND 6 P.M. (ASSUMING YOUR BANK IS OPEN MONDAY THROUGH FRIDAY, 8 A.M. TO 6 P.M.).

WHY? FBI statistics consistently show that Fridays, Mondays, and mornings have the highest number of bank robberies. Afternoons on Tuesdays, Wednesdays, and Thursdays are probably the least likely times for a robbery to occur, putting you at little to no risk of being accosted or losing your money.

⚠ *WORDS OF CAUTION: Common lore says that banks have more cash on hand on Fridays (it being payday) and in the morning. While this is not true, nobody's told the bank robbers.*

WHAT IS THE SAFEST BANK LOCATION?

A RESIDENTIAL NEIGHBORHOOD.

WHY? Most U.S. bank robberies—about 5,000 a year—occur in commercial or urban districts. Residential neighborhoods, by comparison, experience about 500 robberies per year. For the safest option, use a bank inside a supermarket: These branches experience the fewest robberies, since it is considered harder to take control of an entire supermarket than just a bank.

OUTSIDE OR INSIDE A BANK.

WHY? Not only are bank-run ATMs regulated by state banking associations, they're also more likely to be monitored by a guard, a camera, or both. This makes them less attractive to thieves. Privately run ATMs (the kinds in delis, gas stations, and bars) are generally stand-alone and lack monitoring devices. While you might not be approached for cash in a deli, privately run machines are easier to tamper with, allowing high-tech thieves to steal your PIN number and account information.

⚠ *WORDS OF CAUTION: ATM fraud usually involves thieves placing a thin plastic overlay on the keypad to capture your PIN or inserting a device inside the card-swiping slot to record your account information (the kind of slots that "eat" your card are less likely to have been rigged). If the keyboard looks funny, or if the card swipe feels rough or sticky, stop the transaction and find another ATM.*

WHAT IS THE SAFEST TIME TO SEE A FRIEND WHO HAS THE FLU?

SEVEN DAYS AFTER SYMPTOMS START TO SHOW.

WHY? A person's flu can be contagious any time from a day before he shows symptoms to three to seven days after flu-like symptoms (e.g., headache, stiffness, exhaustion, sore throat, runny or stuffy nose) appear.

⚠ *WORDS OF CAUTION:* *A flu sufferer is most contagious from the second to fourth day of infection, so stay away if it's only been a couple of days since his nose started running. If you must be around someone who's sick, be sure to wash your hands frequently; it's your best defense against catching the flu virus.*

ACETAMINOPHEN.

WHY? As long as you take the recommended amount, acetaminophen, best known as Tylenol®, is the safest pain reliever because it isn't as likely to cause stomach bleeding and irritation. In contrast, nonsteroidal anti-inflammatory drugs (NSAIDs), which include ibuprofen, naproxen, and aspirin, cause an increased risk of nausea, ulcers, and kidney problems, especially for people over age 65.

⚠ *WORDS OF CAUTION: Heavy drinkers should avoid acetaminophen because it can increase the severity of liver damage. Aspirin should not be administered to children; it has been linked to Reye's syndrome, a potentially fatal disorder. Use acetaminophen or ibuprofen products instead.*

WHAT IS THE SAFEST TEMPERATURE FOR A HOT TUB?

104°F (40°C) OR BELOW.

WHY? Soaking in a hot tub in which the temperature is too high raises your body temperature, which can raise your blood pressure and lead to heatstroke.

⚠ *WORDS OF CAUTION:* *Be sure to keep your hair tied up while you're bubbling. Since 1978, the U.S. Consumer Product Safety Commission has reported at least 49 injuries, including 13 deaths, among bathers whose hair was sucked into the drain of a spa, hot tub, or whirlpool.*

WHAT IS THE SAFEST AMOUNT OF TIME TO SIT IN A SAUNA?

TEN MINUTES (OR LESS).

WHY? The scorching 180°F (82°C) heat of a sauna can be dangerous if you partake for too long. The longer you sit in the sauna, the greater your chances for dehydration or heatstroke.

⚠ ***WORDS OF CAUTION:*** *Sitting in a sauna can temporarily affect your blood pressure; if you're already taking blood pressure or heart medicine, talk to your doctor before going in. Remember to place a towel on the bench before taking a seat; germs love the sauna's heat and, in a less-than-clean sauna, could be crawling all over the bench.*

WHAT IS THE SAFEST STALL IN A PUBLIC RESTROOM?

THE STALL CLOSEST TO THE DOOR.

WHY? A University of Arizona study of public restrooms found that the stall closest to the door was the one that consistently had the least traffic, and therefore the lowest levels of bacteria.

⚠ ***WORDS OF CAUTION:*** *Avoid the middle stall. It is used the most and therefore is probably contaminated with the most germs. (It will also have the least toilet paper.)*

WHAT IS THE SAFEST WAY TO SIT ON A PUBLIC TOILET?

WIPE IT OFF FIRST, THEN COVER THE SEAT WITH PAPER.

WHY? Toilet seats are generally too dry for most bacteria to survive. The real danger of sitting on the seat is touching any fluids that were left behind by the person before you. Your best bet is to wipe the seat off with a piece of toilet paper or a paper towel before covering it with paper or a commercially designed seat protector.

⚠ **WORDS OF CAUTION:** *Really, the toilet's the last thing you should worry about in a public bathroom. Studies have shown that the door handle and the water tap are far dirtier than the toilet seats, since people tend to carry more germs on their hands than on their behinds. Another warning: Once you flush, get out of the way—thousands of germs are catapulted into the air each time you flush.*

WHAT IS THE SAFEST WAY TO DRY YOUR HANDS IN A PUBLIC RESTROOM?

USING A PAPER TOWEL.

WHY? Paper towels, specifically the kind you grab from a dispenser (as opposed to a roll that could have touched the floor) are your best bets because you know you're the first one to touch them.

⚠ **WORDS OF CAUTION:** *Think hand dryers are safer because you're not touching anything? Think again. Bacteria enjoy higher temperatures and can thrive inside the dryer vents. When you stick your hands beneath them, germs may blow out; the germs can settle on your hands, and you may inhale an unhealthy dose. Be careful what you touch, as well: A University of Arizona study showed that about a quarter of all public bathroom surfaces are contaminated with body fluids, including blood, mucous, urine, or saliva.*

WHAT IS THE SAFEST PART OF THE BODY FOR PIERCING?

THE EARLOBES.

WHY? There's a reason the ears are the most commonly pierced part of the body in the United States. Ear piercings carry relatively low risk; earlobes do not contain dense tissue, take a relatively short time to heal (six to eight weeks), and are less likely to be covered in clothing (covered piercings heal more slowly).

⚠ *WORDS OF CAUTION: Think twice before getting your tongue pierced. Tongue piercings account for some of the most serious piercing complications because the mouth is full of bacteria. An infected tongue has a remote potential to swell up and cut off your airway through the throat. If that isn't enough, the American Dental Association cautions that tongue piercings tend to chip and fracture teeth. If you're hankering for a belly-button ring, get ready for at least a few months of discomfort; navel piercings are prone to infection and take the longest to heal.*

WHAT IS THE SAFEST MONTH TO GET ELECTIVE SURGERY?

JUNE.

WHY? At most hospitals, new residents start their work in July, and many doctors will tell you that it is therefore the most hectic month at the hospital. By June, the residents will have been around for nearly a full year and are potentially more comfortable at the hospital.

⚠ **WORDS OF CAUTION:** *Try to make doctor appointments for first thing in the morning because you are more likely to be seen on time. Avoid Mondays: they're notoriously the busiest day at hospitals and clinics because people tend to put off their problems during the weekend.*

WHAT IS THE SAFEST WAY TO TALK ON A CELL PHONE?

WITH A HEADSET, HOLDING THE PHONE AWAY FROM YOUR BODY.

WHY? There are no scientific data proving that wireless phones are harmful in any way (other than while driving, see below), but there has been concern that the low level of radiation emitted from the phones (the FDA considers it a relatively harmless amount) could accelerate tumor growth. Exposure levels decrease dramatically with distance, so use a headset and keep the phone away from your body.

⚠ **WORDS OF CAUTION:** While there is no conclusive evidence linking radiation and cell phones, it's a well-known fact that driving while talking on a phone can be dangerous. Driving without a hands-free device for your phone is illegal in some states due to its link to accidents. Automobiles aside, talking on a headset is also better for your neck, since you don't have to lean your head into the phone.

SOURCES

Chapter 1: Around the House

What Is the Safest Position for TV Watching?
American Academy of Ophthalmology. • Roselyn Payne Epps, Susan Cobb Steward (editors), The American Medical Women's Association *Women's Complete Healthbook*, 1995.

What Is the Safest Number of Appliances to Plug into an Extension Cord?
"Extension Cords: Not One Size Fits All," Underwriters Laboratories Inc., 2002. • "Dorm Room Safety 101," Underwriters Laboratories Inc., 2002 (www.ul.com). • "Electrical Safety," National Fire Protection Association, 2002 (www.nfpa.org).

What Is the Safest Kind of Landline Phone?
"Safety Information for Short Term Power Outages or Rolling Blackouts," Red Cross. • Roger Williams, "How to Have a Cordless Phone and Maintain Privacy," *The Digital Journalist*, 2003. • Mark Harrington, "Old Technologies Thrive in Blackout," *Newsday*, August 17, 2003.

What Is the Safest Position for Sleeping?
"Information From Your Family Doctor," American Academy of Family Physicians patient information piece, May 2003. • *American Journal of Gastroenterology*, 1999.

What Is the Safest Height to Climb a Ladder?
American Academy of Orthopaedic Surgeons (www.aaos.org).

What Is the Safest Way to Hammer a Nail?
Erik D'Amato, "Taming of the Screw: 25 Strategies for the Safe Use of Hardware Tools," *Men's Health*, November 1995. • "Techniques for Driving and Hiding Nails," Do It Yourself Network (www.diynet.com). • Consumer Product Safety Commission (www.cpsc.gov). • "The Big Picture: Hanging Requires the Right Fastener," *Newsday*, October 1997. • "Quake Country: Making Your Home Safe," *San Francisco Chronicle*, 2003.

What Is the Safest Way to Get Paint off Your Hands?
American Association of Poison Control Centers (www.aapcc.org).

What Is the Safest Way to Protect Your Home Against Burglary?
Federal Bureau of Investigation, 2002 (www.fbi.gov). • National Burglar

and Fire Alarm Association (www.alarm.org).

What Is the Safest Way to Get Rid of Roaches?
Joe Kita, "Pest-Proof Your Life," *Men's Health*, March 2000. • "What Pests Want in Your Home," *National Wildlife*, August 1999.

What Is the Safest Way to Get Rid of Backyard Pests?
Joe Kita, "Pest-Proof Your Life," *Men's Health*, March 2000.
• "Repellency of Plant, Natural Products, and Predator Odors on Woodchucks," United States Department of Agriculture (www.usda.gov).
• ASPCA Animal Poison Control Centers (www.aspca.org/apcc).

What Is the Safest Kind of Lawn Mower?
Consumer Product Safety Commission (www.cpsc.gov). • American Academy of Ophthalmology (www.aao.org).

Chapter 2: In the Kitchen

What Is the Safest Temperature at Which to Set Your Refrigerator?
Food Safety and Inspection Service, United States Department of Agriculture (www.fsis.usda.gov).

What Is the Safest Amount of Time to Keep Leftovers in the Refrigerator?
Food Safety and Inspection Service, United States Department of Agriculture (www.fsis.usda.gov).

What Is the Safest Amount of Time to Let Food Sit on the Counter?
Partnership for Food Safety Education, United States Department of Agriculture (www.foodsafety.gov).

What Is the Safest Amount of Time to Store Canned Foods?
Food Safety and Inspection Service, United States Department of Agriculture (www.fsis.usda.gov). • Centers for Disease Control and Prevention (www.cdc.gov).

What Is the Safest Way to Clean the Kitchen Counter?
Food Safety and Inspection Service (www.fsis.usda.gov). • United States Department of Agriculture (www.fsis.usda.gov).

What Is the Safest Amount of Time to Keep a Sponge?
American Society for Microbiology (www.asm.org). • Partnership for Food Safety Education, United States Department of Agriculture (www.foodsafety.gov).

What Is the Safest Kind of Cutting Board?
Food and Drug Administration Center for Food Safety and Applied Nutrition (http://vm.cfsan.fda.gov).

What Is the Safest Kind of Home Fire Extinguisher?
"Product Safety Tips: Household Fire Extinguishers," Underwriters Laboratories Inc., 2003 (www.ul.com). • National Fire Protection Association (www.nfpa.org).

Chapter 3: Food and Drink

What Is the Safest Way to Defrost Meat?
Food and Drug Administration's Center for Food Safety and Applied Nutrition (http//vm.cfsan.fda.gov). • Food Safety and Inspection Service, United States Department of Agriculture (www.fsis.usda.gov).

What Is the Safest Way to Barbecue?
U.S. Fire Administration (www.usfa.fema.gov). • Consumer Product Safety Commission (www.cpsc.gov).

What Is the Safest Way to Cook a Hamburger?
Food Safety and Inspection Service, United States Department of Agriculture (www.fsis.usda.gov).

What Is the Safest Kind of Raw Fish?
Michael Jahncke, center director at the Virginia Seafood Agricultural Research and Extension Center. • Food and Drug Administration Center for Food Safety and Applied Nutrition (http://vm.cfsan.fda.gov). • California Poison Control System (www.calpoison.org). • "Buy It Fresh, Keep It Fresh," *Consumer Reports*, February 2001.

What Is the Safest Kind of Fruit?
Environmental Protection Agency (www.epa.gov). • Environmental Working Group, "2003 Report Card: Pesticides in Produce."

What Is the Safest Kind of Bottled Water?

"Preventing Cryptosporidiosis: A Guide to Water Filters and Bottled Water," Centers for Disease Control and Prevention (www.cdc.gov), November 2002. • "Bottled Water: Pure Drink or Pure Hype?" National Resources Defense Council, 1999 (www.nrdc.org). • "Bottled and Distilled Water," U.S. Environmental Protection Agency (www.epa.gov). • Amy Powell, Big Geyser, Inc.

What Is the Safest Way to Drink from a Soda Can?

April Austin, "Clean Your Soda Can Before You Take a Sip," KOVR 13 CBS, February 20, 2001. • Philip M. Tierno Jr., Ph.D., director of clinical microbiology and immunology, associate professor, departments of microbiology and pathology at New York University Medical Center, and author of *The Secret Life of Germs: Observations and Lessons from a Microbe Hunter*, Pocket Books, 2001.

What Is the Safest Amount of Caffeine to Allow in Your Diet?

National Institutes of Health (www.nih.gov). • American Dietetic Association (www.eatright.org/Public). • U.S. Food and Drug Administration (www.fda.gov). • National Soft Drink Association (www.nsda.org). • American Medical Association (www.ama-assn.org). • Coffee Science Information Center's Coffee and Caffeine Health Information (www.cosic.org).

What Is the Safest Artificial Sweetener?

FDA Consumer, U.S. Food and Drug Administration, November–December 1999. • American Dietetic Association (www.eatright.org/Public). • "Cancer Facts: Artificial Sweeteners," National Cancer Institute (www.cancer.gov). • "Saccharin Should Not Have Been Delisted," Center for Science in the Public Interest, May 15, 2000. • Michael D. Lemonick, "How Safe Are the Sugar Substitutes? Artificial Sweeteners Are More Popular Than Ever—but Questions Persist," *Time*, September 15, 2003. • "Food Allergies Rare but Risky," *FDA Consumer*, U.S. Food and Drug Administration, May 1994.

What Is the Safest Way to Open a Bottle of Champagne?

American Academy of Ophthalmology (www.aao.org).

Chapter 4: In the Bathroom

What Is the Safest Way to Bathe?
Consumer Product Safety Commission (www.cpsc.gov).

What Is the Safest Way to Wash Your Hands?
Dr. Charles Gerba, microbiologist, University of Arizona. • Philip M. Tierno Jr., Ph.D., director of clinical microbiology and immunology, associate professor, departments of microbiology and pathology at New York University Medical Center, and author of *The Secret Life of Germs: Observations and Lessons from a Microbe Hunter*, Pocket Books, 2001. • "Antibacterial Household Products: Cause for Concern," Centers for Disease Control and Prevention (www.cdc.gov), *Emerging Infectious Diseases Journal*, June 2001.

What Is the Safest Place to Store Your Toothbrush?
"Infection Control: The Use and Handling of Toothbrushes," Centers for Disease Control and Prevention (www.cdc.gov) Fact Sheet, January 2002. • "Is Your Family Sharing Too Much?" The Academy of General Dentistry (www.agd.org), 2003.

What Is the Safest Number of Times to Use a Disposable Razor?
Debra Jaliman, MD, board-certified dermatologist, clinical instructor at Mount Sinai Hospital, and media spokesperson for the American Academy of Dermatology (www.aad.org).

What Is the Safest Way to Color Your Hair?
Alicia Di Rado, "USC Study Points to Bladder Cancer Risk from Long-Term Hair Dye Use," University of California Keck School of Medicine, January 2001. • Ridgely Ochs, "To Color or Not to Color: Though a Recent Study on Cancer and Hair Dye Is Reassuring, the Question Still Isn't a Simple One," *Newsday*, February 28, 1994.

Chapter 5: Man's Best Friend

What Is the Safest Way to Meet a Dog?
Victoria Stilwell, dog trainer of 10 years, currently at Dog Trainers of New York (www.dogtrainersofnewyork.com).

What Is the Safest Kind of Over-the-Counter Pain Reliever to Give a Dog?
"Care and Nurturing of Cats," Food and Drug Administration Center for Veterinary Medicine. • "The Medicine Chest," Petsmart.com, 1996.

What Is the Safest Way to Transport a Pet?
"ASPCA Warns Pet Owners About Hazards of Transporting Pets," American Society for the Prevention of Cruelty to Animals (www.aspca.org) press release, November 15, 2002. • Carolyn Spencer Brown, "On the Road with Fifi and Fido," *The Washington Post*, June 17, 2001. • "Traveling by Car with Your Pet," American Animal Hospital Association (www.healthypet.com).

Chapter 6: Sports and Entertainment

What Is the Safest Spectator Professional Sport?
Liz Chandler, "Auto Racing Death Toll Is Surprisingly High, Investigation Finds," Knight Ridder/Tribune News Service, November 9, 2001. • Mike Harris, "How Safe Are Auto Races for Spectators," Associated Press, July 28, 1998. • Hal Habib, "Message to Spectators: Watch Out, You're at Risk," *Palm Beach Post*, March 24, 2002. • "Girl Killed By Stray Hockey Puck," CBS News, March 20, 2002.

What Is the Safest Seat at a Major-League Baseball Game?
James Kozlowski, "Spectators Assume Obvious Risks in Unprotected Areas of Ballfield," *NRPA Law Review*, April 1997. • Neil Goldberg, sports producer, *New York One News.* Hal Habib, "Message to Spectators: Watch Out, You're at Risk," *Palm Beach Post*, March 24, 2002.

What Is the Safest Seat at a Professional Hockey Game?
Neil Goldberg, sports producer, *New York One News.* • General Information Office, Madison Square Garden. • "Nets to Hang at Arenas," Associated Press, June 20, 2002. • James C. Kozlowski, J.D., Ph.D., "Hockey Puck 'Facial' a Foreseeable Risk for Spectators?" *NRPA Law Review*, August, 1998. • "View Obstructions Are an Inherent Risk of Attending a Sporting Event," *California Case Comments*, December 2002. • Michael Farber, "Put Up the Net: Spectators Don't Want Their Views Obstructed, but Protecting Fans, as European Leagues Do,

Should Be an NHL Priority," *Sports Illustrated*, April 1, 2002. • Ira Dreyfuss, "Sports Fans in Stands Face Risks," Associated Press, March 24, 2002.

What Is the Safest Seat at an Auto Race?
"How Safe Are Auto Races for Spectators," Associated Press, July 28, 1998. • Jeff Hinton, Public Relations, Daytona International Speedway.

What Is the Safest Piece of Gym Equipment?
American Sports Data Inc. 2003. • Kevin Makely, New York City personal trainer, competitive body builder, and fitness expert for Bally's Total Fitness.

What Is the Safest Seat at a Concert?
Anthony DeBarros, "Concertgoers' Push Injuries Surge to High Levels Decades After Deadly Who Show, Violence Worsens," *USA Today*, July 8, 2000. • Paul Wertheimer, "Rock Concert Safety Survey," Crowd Management Strategies, 2002.

What Is the Safest Kind of Fireworks?
"Use Fireworks Safely," National Safety Council (www.nsc.org), June 2002. • "Fireworks-Related Injuries," Centers for Disease Control and Prevention (www.cdc.gov), 2002.

What Is the Safest Amusement Park Ride?
Joel L. Cliff, technical writer, International Association of Amusement Parks and Attractions (www.iaapa.org). • "Amusement Ride-Related Injuries and Deaths in the United States, 1987–2000," Consumer Product Safety Commission (www.cpsc.gov).

What Is the Safest Piece of Playground Equipment?
"Playground Safety: Injuries," Centers for Disease Control and Prevention (www.cdc.gov). • "Playground Safety," National Safety Council, 2003.

Chapter 7: Travel and the Great Outdoors

What Is the Safest Kind of Hotel?
"U.S. Airport Hotels Are Safest, Most Secure, Cornell Expert Finds," Cornell University Center for Hospitality Research, September 2002.

What Is the Safest Room in a Hotel?

"U.S. Airport Hotels Are Safest, Most Secure, Cornell Expert Finds," Cornell University Center for Hospitality Research, September 2002. • Gary Lee, "Hotels Exposed; Cost of Little Soaps? Adult Movies? We Asked for It," *The Washington Post*, June 3, 2001.

What Is the Safest Way to Sleep in a Motel Bed?

Sylvia Chase, Diane Sawyer, Sam Donaldson, "Clean Sweep," *ABC PrimeTime Live*, March 24, 1998. • Michel Mousseau, hotel inspector for the American Automobile Association (www.aaa.com).

What Is the Safest Place to Pitch a Tent?

Great Outdoor Recreation Pages (GORP, http://gorp.away.com).

What Is the Safest Way to Swim in the Ocean?

International Shark Attack File, University of Florida Museum of Natural History.

What Is the Safest City in the United States?

Morgan Quitno Awards (www.morganquitno.com). • "Preliminary Uniform Crime Reports," Federal Bureau of Investigation (www.fbi.gov), January–December 2002. • "Amherst N.Y. Safest City, Magazine Says," Associated Press, November 26, 1996. • John Moslow, Amherst, New York, Chief of Police.

What Is the Safest City for Air Quality in the United States?

"State of the Air 2003: Grading the Risk in America's 25 Most-Ozone-Polluted Cities," American Lung Association (www.lungusa.org).

Where Is the Safest Place When Outdoors During a Lightning Storm?

National Weather Service Office of Climate, Weather, and Water Services (www.nws.noaa.gov/om).

Where Is the Safest Place When Indoors During a Lightning Storm?

National Weather Service Office of Climate, Weather, and Water Services (www.nws.noaa.gov/om).

What Is the Safest Place to Be During a Tornado?

Federal Emergency Management Agency (www.fema.gov). • Centers for Disease Control and Prevention (www.cdc.org). • Chris Cappella,

"Overpasses Are Tornado Death Traps," *USA Today*, May 15, 2003.

What Is the Safest Place to Be During a Hurricane?
Federal Emergency Management Agency (www.fema.gov).

Chapter 8: Planes, Trains, and Automobiles

What Is the Safest Kind of Flight to Take?
"Aviation Safety Data Accessibility Study Index: Safety Data," Federal Aviation Administration Office of System Safety (www1.faa.gov).

What Is the Safest Kind of Plane?
"Top Ten Airline Safety Tips," www.Airsafe.com. • Todd Curtis, airline safety analyst for the Boeing Company, 1991 to 2000. • "Aviation Safety Data Accessibility Study Index: Analysis and Interpretation of Safety Data," Federal Aviation Administration Office of System Safety (www1.faa.gov). • "Annual Review of Aircraft Accident Data," National Transportation Safety Board (www.ntsb.gov).

What Is the Safest Location on a Plane?
Charles Chittum, "In His Own Words: Crash Course—Even If Your Plane Goes Down, Says an Expert, There May Be Simple Things You Can Do to Survive," *People*, October 20, 1997. • Margaret Loftus, "Finding the Safest Airline Seat," *U.S. News & World Report*, May 11, 1998.

What Is the Safest Form of Mass Transit?
"Transit Safety and Security Statistics and Analysis Report: Traffic Safety Data by Mode for All Reported Incidents," U.S. Department of Transportation, Federal Transit Administration (www.fta.dot.gov), 2000.

What Is the Safest Car on a Train?
Department of Transportation (www.dot.gov). • Metropolitan Transportation Authority (www.mta.nyc.ny.us).

What Is the Safest Type of Car to Drive?
Insurance Institute for Highway Safety. • U.S. Department of Transportation National Highway Traffic Safety Administration.

What Is the Safest Seat in a Car?
U.S. Department of Transportation's Fatality Analysis Reporting System, 2002.

What Is the Safest Driving Lane?
Joe Younger, American Automobile Association (www.aaa.com), 2003.

What Is the Safest Day of the Week to Go for a Drive?
"Traffic Safety Facts," U.S. Department of Transportation, National Highway Traffic and Safety Administration (www.nhtsa.dot.gov), 2001.

What Is the Safest Color Car to Drive?
"Bus and Passenger Accident Prevention," U.S. Department of Transportation, Federal Transit Agency (www.nhtsa.dot.gov), 1999. • "Car Color and Safety," American Automobile Association (www.aaa.com) Foundation for Vehicle Safety, 2003. • "Lime-Yellow Fire Trucks Safer Than Red: A Conclusion from Four Years of Data," TranSafety, Inc., 1997.

What Is the Safest Place to Pull Over When Stopped by an Unmarked Police Car?
Casey Perry, Chairman of the National State Troopers Coalition.

What Is the Safest Place to Park in a Parking Garage?
Tome Squitieri, "The Dangers Down Under Trigger Building Code Changes," *USA Today*, July 18, 1995.

What Is the Safest State to Drive in?
American Automobile Association (www.aaa.com). • National Safety Council, 2000 (www.nsc.org).

Chapter 9: Everyday Safety

What Is the Safest Time to Go to the Bank?
Federal Bureau of Investigation (www.fbi.gov).

What Is the Safest Bank Location?
Federal Bureau of Investigation (www.fbi.gov).

What Is the Safest ATM Location?
John Hall, public relations representative with the American Bankers Association. • "Private ATM Machines May Be Targets for Thieves," *New York One News*, November 6, 2003.

What Is the Safest Time to See a Friend Who Has the Flu?
"Influenza Questions and Answers," Centers for Disease Control and

Prevention (www.cdc.org). • Michelle Meadows, "Beat the Winter Bugs: How to Hold Your Own Against Colds and Flu," U.S. Food and Drug Administration (www.fda.gov), *FDA Consumer Magazine*, November–December 2001.

What Is the Safest Kind of Pain Reliever?
Craig Josephs, emergency room doctor, New York City. • *Journal of Emergency Medicine*, 2002. • "Use Caution With Pain Relievers," *FDA Consumer Magazine*, January–February 2003. • "What are NSAIDs?" American Academy of Orthopedic Surgeons (www.aaos.org).

What Is the Safest Temperature for a Hot Tub?
Consumer Product Safety Commission (www.cpsc.gov), "Spas, Hot Tubs, and Whirlpools," 2001.

What Is the Safest Amount of Time to Sit in a Sauna?
Heather Morgan, "The Heat Is On: The Safety Factor Behind Steam Rooms, Saunas, and Whirlpools," www.GymAmerica.com.

What Is the Safest Stall in a Public Restroom?
Stephanie Allmon, "Avoiding Bathroom Bacteria Is in Your Hands," *The Washington Times*, February 13, 2000. • "Behind the Bathroom Door," *Men's Health*, March 2002. • "Stalling Tactics: How to Use Public Washrooms but Avoid Public Bacteria," *Prevention*, November 1997.

What Is the Safest Way to Sit on a Public Toilet?
Dr. Charles Gerba, "Microorganisms in Public Washrooms," 1995. • Dru Sefton, "Toilet Seats Get a Bum Rap," Newhouse News Service, July 2003. • Stephanie Allmon, "Avoiding Bathroom Bacteria Is in Your Hands," *The Washington Times*, February 13, 2000.

What Is the Safest Way to Dry Your Hands in a Public Restroom?
Dr. Charles Gerba, University of Arizona, "Microorganisms in Public Washrooms," 1995.

What Is the Safest Part of the Body for Piercing?
Debra Jaliman, MD, board-certified dermatologist, clinical instructor at Mount Sinai Hospital, and media spokesperson for the American Academy of Dermatology (www.aad.org). • Myrna L. Armstrong, "You Pierced What?" *Pediatric Nursing*, May–June 1996. • "Oral Piercing and Health," *Journal of the American Dental Association*, January 2001.

What Is the Safest Month to Get Elective Surgery?
Craig Josephs, emergency room doctor, New York City.

What Is the Safest Way to Talk on a Cell Phone?
Doug Dollemore, "Cell Phone Safety News," *Prevention*, March 2002.
• "Cell Phone Facts: Consumer Information on Wireless Phones," Food and Drug Administration, July 2003 (www.fda.gov/cellphones).

First of all, I'd like to thank David Borgenicht for letting me tirelessly pester him until we finally found the right idea. And to Erin Slonaker, my editor, for making the whole process so strangely simple. I thank designer Karen Onorato and illustrator Willie Ryan for turning lots of everyday things into a catchy little package. I also owe thanks to all the sources who contributed their expertise to this book, without whom I'd have never started doing things like wiping off my soda can before I take a sip.

Also, I promised my bosses, Marc Nathanson and Kevin Dugan, at *New York One News,* that I'd thank them for giving me some time off—and during the black-out, no less. Thanks, guys (glad I missed the blackout).

And thanks to all my friends, roommates, family members, and coworkers for dealing with my never-ending tirade of anxieties. These people include: My parents, Virginia Biddle, Elizabeth Krow, Alexis Cairns, Tony Crane, Emily Clark, Lucy Reading, Amy Powell, Karen Fuhrman, Dustin Stephens, Sandra Mariano, Gary Cazzaretti, Jeslyn Kelly, John Hartzell, Monique Leigh, Larry Pryor, Deanna Williams, Christian Unruh, Shelley Preston, Jason Novak, Jordan Burchette, and Colin Miner.

Turns out, all that worrying is good for something.